I0781390

REPUBLICAN 101

A PRIMER ON BEING A REPUBLICAN IN THE U.S. OF A.

By David Lay

Author Bio: Semi-retired, David Lay, a chemical physicist, lives on his farm in central Missouri. David grew up in a conservative Republican household; his mother a librarian, his father a chemist; both parents raised on farms in the Midwest.

ISBN: 9781724098801

South Farm Publishing, LLC

PO Box 58

Graff, Missouri 65660

While the author has made good effort to provide accurate URL addresses for websites cited at the time of publication, neither he nor the publisher assumes responsibility for errors or changes that occur after publication, nor does the publisher have any control over and does not assume any responsibility for, and any content therein, any author or third party websites or social media pages.

Cover photo credit: David Lay

South Farm Logo: Ryan Jones, Queensland, Australia

Acknowledgements, Footnotes and References:

I will not make footnotes for references within the text, but will list a bibliography from where I have taken my facts and information at the end. I must admit I depended very heavily on Wikipedia, though not wholly on them, who are honest to say whether or not a posting may or may not be fully vetted, and they also list the latest updates. When dealing with historical information, I find their posts reliable, and much of what you read in this primer has depended on information gleaned from those good folks. I would encourage anyone who has used Wikipedia to donate to their cause to keep such a wonderful service available.

I do hope that those reading this will look at the reference materials I've listed. I do, indeed, "...stand upon the shoulders of giants..." while I write this. I give my grateful thanks to the many historians, journalists, and political scientists, *et al.* upon whom I've depended, not just in preparing for this primer, but during my life's pursuits, to write this primer.

I am not a historian. I was trained as a scientist, and I know, from taking a course in how historians get and assimilate their information and forming as accurate a depiction of history as is possible, putting together history is a form of science itself, and a difficult science at that.

If you should find error in my writing, references, or logic, please write me a *kind* letter, correcting me and my transgressions, giving references as you do so. I will make corrections and changes in future editions. Author

"The truth unquestionably is, that the only path to a subversion of the republican system of the country is, by flattering the prejudices of the people, and exciting their jealousies and apprehensions, to throw affairs into confusion, and bring on civil commotion...

**When a man unprincipled in private life...
desperate in his fortune, bold in his temper,
possessed of considerable talents... despotic in his
ordinary demeanor – known to have scoffed in
private at the principles of liberty – when such a
man is seen to mount the hobby horse of popularity
– to join in the cry of danger to liberty – to take
every opportunity of embarrassing the General
Government & bringing it under suspicion – to
flatter and fall in with all the non sense of the
zealots of the day – it may justly be suspected that
his object is to throw things into confusion that he
may 'ride the storm and direct the whirlwind'"**

Alexander Hamilton, *Objections and Answers Respecting the Administration*, August 18,1782

(A more complete quote of this excerpt may be found in the Appendix)

Table of Contents

INTRODUCTION: WHAT DO YOU MEAN; YOU'RE A "REPUBLICAN"?

"A Republic, Madam, if we can keep it"

Benjamin Franklin, 1787

I was talking to the fellow who helps me on my farm one day, and during our conversation he made the statement "There's gonna be a race war, and I'm gonna be on the front lines." This man declares himself to be a Republican, as do ninety percent plus of the folks around here. He only watches Fox News, as do most of the folks around here, and quotes them with regularity. If he were computer literate he might watch CRTV on the internet. He listens only to the conservative talking heads, such as Rush Limbaugh, *et allii (Latin for "and others")*, and sees no wrong in their logic. The "demoncraps" are the enemy; they're all socialists, or, worse, communists, and "all of 'em should be lined up against a wall and shot". He believes Obama is a foreigner and has caused all of our problems. He sees the "government" as "them" or "they", and believes the government is essentially evil; he believes all public institutions, such as public schools, should be abolished. He thinks we should be flying the Confederate flag… This man is not a Republican as I have known them, I having been raised in a Republican household.

Over all, this man is a good man; he works hard, doing work that would lay out most folks. He is faithful to his invalid wife, taking care of her in ways that would make most of us send her off to a nursing home; but his statements confound me: It is obvious that the definitions of the politics of this country have become skewed within the last thirty plus years. I'd even be so bold to say beginning since Reagan first took office, and many people who *claim* to be Republicans seem to have lost what it truly, originally meant to be a Republican.

This man's opinions are an indicator, a thermometer of what is happening nation-wide. There has become a mean and angry discord between the two main political parties and this discord begins in the microcosms of local communities and extends to the national government, with each faction moving toward the extremes of our society's beliefs.

I, like my father, am afraid of this kind of extremism that has taken hold in our government: A relative minority (may I venture to say about ten to fifteen percent of the population) of the extreme factions of our society *have taken control of our government, imposing their beliefs on the majority of the populous, moving away from the political moderation of most within our society.*

This *primer* is meant to set the record straight; to define the limits of the moderate majority and to define the true Republican. It also will attempt to offer some kind of fix, albeit perhaps naïve, for what I perceive as a broken political system. I purposely made this book short, so please bear with me and please read it to the end.

Wouldn't it be nice if people knew what they are saying when they called themselves a *Republican…*

I should know: I was raised in a conservative, and Republican, household. My parents were religious. They married late as did their parents; my grandfather was born in 1873, my mother in 1912, and both my grandparents had farms. While growing up I heard many "pioneer" stories from people who had lived through those hard times, stories of the Dust Bowl in Oklahoma and the Great Depression. My great-grandfather fought for the Confederacy. In all that time I never heard any racist remarks from anyone in my family. If anyone had reason to have strong and biased beliefs, it was them; but they didn't, at least not that I was aware of. If they had those beliefs, they hid them well. My father, raised on a successful farm, was a chemist, and my mother, raised on a farm caught in the Dust Bowl in Oklahoma, and hence having grown up in poverty, was a librarian.

My parents were involved in local politics and in the community, and my father was very troubled at the rise of the *John Birch Society*, an ultra-conservative organization formed in the late 1950's, and saw that organization's extremism dangerous. My parents were, in my opinion, some of the last, true, Republicans...

We, the citizens of *the* United States of America, are in for a lot of trouble if we do not buffer our strong and often wrong and mislead viewpoints.

This Nation

The United States of America, which, *through the introduction of faulty policies by unethical leaders, poisoned by unethical media,* is being sent into an untenable and economic oblivion… There is danger ahead…

-There is danger from the "he said, she said", "some say", and *innuendo* journalism. This is, very simply, misinformation and propaganda. Propaganda is dangerous, especially if those seeing or hearing it cannot, or will not, discern the difference between propaganda, misinformation, and truth (see the "7 Ways to Recognize Propaganda" by Edward Filene in the Appendix). *People who have never been educated in, or do not take the time to approach political discourse with trepidation, discerning embedded untruths in their information, and not checking the facts as they go, are especially vulnerable to this kind of propaganda.*

-There is danger in the "win at any cost" attitudes and the "crony" politics of the two main political parties, using methods within the political system to "cheat", giving their party the advantage over the other; *Gerrymandering* is an example of this.

-There is danger in the "name calling" that has evolved: It would horrify those who grew up in the 1930's and 40's if they knew that *newspeak*, a term that comes out of the novel *1984*, by Orson Wells, written in the 1930's, has become the language of the new, corporate news conglomerates, the "spinners" of political bias from both the Democrats and the Republicans, and even so called *memes* posted on social media pages.

-There is danger from those who dominate social and main stream media and have redefined "right" and "left", "Conservatives" and "Liberals", to such names as "Repugs" and "Demoncraps", or worse, and who, by doing so, are separating

the factions even farther apart by virtue of a mean and angry *semantics*, using *misdirection* and *misinformation* as tools of manipulating the masses… *It may help a particular faction in the short term, but it will undo all of us in the long term.*

-*There is danger* from the new online news-feeds, both from the right and the left, who are becoming more radical as their audiences coagulate around "hearing what they want to hear": Online news "TV" channels are as *far right* as are the *far left* they criticize, and vice versa. They have become very good at making their statements "believable": It isn't that they are lying and telling untruths so much as they are leaving, carefully it seems, so much out of the balance; and in that they also do so with the hint of drama, drawing in those who revel in gossip. No doubt, too, they are saying much that is simply not true, knowing few will fact check what is said.

Beware of strangers bearing "false" or "fake" news…

Would not a father warn his children not to take candy from a stranger? Why, then, would any parent allow their children to listen to strangers on social media, let alone listen to it themselves? …T*here are a lot of strangers out there luring us into their proverbial "plain white vans" of false ideas, and they use social media to enter into our lives through the posts by, and as, our online "friends".*

To Heal a Nation…

This primer is not intended to preach any religion or creed. It is an attempt to begin a healing of our Nation... albeit a very small attempt, should anyone take the time to read it.

This starts first and foremost by understanding our *Founding Fathers*, what they believed, and what happened between about 100 years before the American Revolution, to the year of the Constitutional Convention, 1787, and to now; also, it is important that we define what and who the political parties are and what they represent.

This primer is structured to first look at the history of how the term "Republican" entered into our national vocabulary, then the evolution of the Republican Party. Last, I will try to define what is wrong with our political system, perhaps naively so, and then how to try to fix it.

This book is part my opinion, part what I learned from some pretty smart people, like David McCullough (a real historian… I suggest you read his book "1776"), *et al.*, and part the thoughts and beliefs of those who came before me, like:

-Our "Founding Fathers"; you know, those guys who said "All men are created equal"….

-And Orson Wells; M' man, if you only knew the truths you have spoken…

-And Benjamin Franklin; your words give us a new and modern challenge....

"...if we can keep it."

"There was truth and there was untruth, and if you clung to the truth even against the whole world, you were not mad."

George Orwell, *Nineteen Eighty-Four,* 1949

CHAPTER 1: WHAT OUR FOUNDING FATHERS BELIEVED

"We mean our guardians to be true saviors"

Plato *The Republic,* Book IV

Few of us, especially any Republicans from my or my parents' generation, do not know of the famous statement made by Benjamin Franklin to a woman at the conclusion of the 1787 Constitutional Convention when she asked "Well, Doctor, what have we got, a Republic or a Monarchy?"

"A republic, madam, if we can keep it," said Ben.

Ol' Ben was correct, except this new Republic was unlike others that came before it: For one thing, it lacked a monarchical leader (a King or Queen). For another, it was made to take the best of other republics either at the time or from times and nations past and improve on them, and in fact it did.

To understand why Benjamin Franklin believed his statement to be true is to be found in understanding who the men were who "forged a new nation".

Our Founding Fathers:

Our Founding Fathers, the people who wrote our Constitution in 1787 to form a new nation, were, most of them, from the elite of society of that day. When I say "elite", I mean this in a good way, in a classical sense: Most (better than half of them) were well-educated… "Classically educated", *id est* (that's Latin for "that is"), they learned, *ad nauseam* (that's Latin for "so much so they were sick of it"), Latin, Greek, usually before they attended college or university, and then, depending on the school they attended, English literature, music, World and ancient history, mathematics, and a general study of the sciences. Thirty out of the fifty five of the delegates to the Constitution Convention had college degrees. *Elite* is not a bad word as some would want you to believe in today's rhetoric. In 1787, the elite were, for the most part, the "good guys".

They, the Founding Fathers, read, and often, because they had to, memorized, Latin and Greek classics in the original languages in which they were written; philosophies, plays, essays, etc. It is no stretch to say the Founding Fathers were some pretty smart fellas… and they were the few. Most people in the new Colonies had little to no education…

…and this fact is very important to understand before we go on: *The ones who founded our country were members of the "elite" within their society...*

Most of the Founding Fathers were educated either in England or in the few schools available in the Colonies at the time, including William and Mary, Yale and Harvard… Their educations were rigorous, and *encouraged argument and discussion…*

As part of their education, they studied the Greek philosophers. Their favorite philosopher was *Plato*, and especially his most popular work (even in Plato's day) the compiled books titled *The Republic…*

...Their favorite play, which they would see multiple times, just like we like to watch our favorite movies over and over, was the play *Cato* by Joseph Addison, written in 1712; a play about the very *ethical* and *moral* Roman Senator, *Cato the Younger*, who was in the Senate at the same time Julius Caesar was in power. His birth name was Marcus Porcius Cato Uticensis who eventually led an unsuccessful civil war against Julius Caesar, who Cato considered, correctly, to be corrupt.

The Founding Fathers' *ideal* governments were the governments of the city states, Rome and Athens; Republics, both. In the ideals of those ancient city states are found the makings of our government today: It was the intention of our fore-fathers to model our government on those ideals, especially from the writings of Plato, where a select group of moral and ethical *guardians, chosen by election* by the citizens, would be who ran the workings of an ideal government *truly for the good of the people.*

In the Founding Fathers ideal government, unethical people would have no place in our new government.

They also had read and were followers of the ideals of a Frenchman named *Baron De Montesquieu*, who studied the attributes of democracies and republics throughout history and the world. He compared, dissected, and categorized those governments, listing their advantages and their faults. Of anyone, Montesquieu probably had the most influence on how the Founding Fathers developed the Constitution. Montesquieu, by modern definition, was a *political scientist.*

Among other writers that influenced the development of our Constitution, the top influencers were *John Locke, Samuel Adams, and Thomas Paine*.

The Founding Fathers, especially those who studied law, were also familiar with the Magna Carta, the use of Common Law, and the evolution of powers within the British government.

So, between Montesquieu, other writers including Locke, Adams, Paine, the British model, the historical contributions of the ancient republics, and Plato's writings, it was very clear to the Founding Fathers that the ***leaders of our new country should be ethical people***, standing above reproach, and should be trusted to run our government for the average citizen in their stead. *Note I have written ethical instead of moral.* I'll explain the differences later.

This is important…

Religion and what the Founding Fathers believed…

This section may *rankle* some readers' religious sensibilities, but *it must be understood what lead the Founding Fathers to "forge" a lasting and effective Constitution*: Up until not much less than one hundred years before the year of the Constitutional Convention, 1787, people who knew religious persecution were still reeling from England's cleansing of Catholicism, Lutheranism, and the new protestant religions such as the Puritans and the Quakers.

Within these religious settlements in early America, *those same religions that were persecuted in England eventually imposed their own forms of persecutions and intolerance within their own colonies*;

An example: The colony of Massachusetts, being a harsh Puritan settlement, considered other religions blasphemous to their beliefs, and people of any other religions were usually exiled, if not harshly punished or executed… In contrast the colony of Maryland, being a Catholic settlement, demanded religious tolerance only because they were barely tolerated by the Protestants across the bay in Virginia, a colony that required by law all residents to attend Anglican services.

Among these more common religions were several smaller religious sects evolving their own form of Christianity, such as the Quakers, not to mention the persecution most of these religions held toward non-Christian religions.

The disparity of religions within the new colonies required a *religious tolerance* if the new government were to survive, and that, then, ***required, among other reasons, the complete and total separation of religion, church, and government***.

Therefore, though most of the Founding Fathers were religious, ***they knew it important that the government be kept separate from religion.*** … the well know "separation of church and state"… But it was even more than that…

Ethics *vs* Morality

The Founding Fathers were religious, but they were considered, and considered themselves, to be *deists*, a common belief at the time: They believed that an Omnipotent being, God, created the Universe, wound it up like a clock, and then let it go to see what happened… *Things happened because mankind made those things happen, not because any god was intervening.*

Though most of the Founding Fathers were religious as such, and they believed in God, they also knew a thing or two about *logic*, and in that light they looked upon religion as a sort of mythical philosophy, much like Greek mythology. It served its purpose in providing a basis for morality, but *had little place in the logistics of developing policy for a nation…*

The founding fathers well understood that allowing religion into government was a set up to allow a particular bias to be the basis for policy; good for some, bad for most, especially for those not of that religion…

Alliis in verbis (Latin for "in other words"), religion and government should not mix… ever. By the Founding Fathers reckoning *government should only be based on logic and ethics*: Morality belongs in religion… ***Ethics belongs in government.***

Exemplar gratis (Latin for "Let me give you an example"): What if a particular religion, let's say a non-Christian religion, that believed only certain humans, given some kind of divine providence, could be the leaders and everyone else should be their slaves, gained control of the government and imposed or forced their beliefs on you? You wouldn't like that very much, would you…

Instead, using ethics and logic as a basis of government *sans* (French for "without") religion, the Constitution was constructed in the light of Plato's model of *the Republic…*

Plato's Republic, the model for our new Republic, and how our government was designed…

As already stated, the Founding Fathers were very familiar with Plato's books, *The Republic*, and the structure of the ancient Roman and Greek governments. They saw it as a basic model, a *starting point*, for developing a *new, modern government*, where, essentially, the people selected, by election, *from members of the elite* to represent them in a *Senate* (a council of educated, ethical men who would make decisions for the country and its well-being)…

It was in this light that the Founding Fathers set down in writing, after much discussion and argument, our beloved *Constitution*. It was a document that was purposely left a bit skimpy, compared to other constitutions, laying down only the *basic formulations* for a workable government. This vagueness is what makes our Constitution flexible and so powerful a tool for a workable government.

The Constitution also gives some hints to how the elite were the ones writing it; *e.g.*, though the people were voting, the elite, especially Thomas Jefferson, believed that some areas with less population should carry the same weight in decisions as areas of more population (otherwise, the more populated areas would always be voting in the government leaving the folks out "in the sticks" with essentially no vote)…

…Makes sense, but also behind this was their underlying belief the uneducated people could not be trusted, for lack of education, to choose correctly; so an *electoral college* was written into the Constitution when the President is to be elected in the stead of the common man, based on the votes from the common people…

…If a member of the Electoral College did not agree with the vote of the poorly educated people he represented, then he could vote how he thought the people, very often his neighbors, should have voted.

The Constitution also allowed for the use of "helpers", those who supported the lawmakers and decision makers by several means: A *cabine*t for the President, *aide*s for the lawmakers, and *bureaucracies* for implementing the policies.

This essentially created something akin to the "three classes of people" stated in Plato's Republic: The Elite, The Helpers to the Elite, and the Workers (the people themselves).

Fortunately, there were some among the Founders that realized the people were to be given a greater respect than that set out in *The Republic*… so it was Benjamin Franklin's idea (actually he proposed a constitution, as such, for the colonies in the 1750's), similar to the House of Commons in British Parliament, and promoted by Alexander Hamilton, to include a *House of Representatives*, the part of the legislative branch that allows *common people* within *districts* to be *directly elected* to represent specific districts (locales) throughout the country… giving more direct votes and weight to the common people… much more like a democracy (I'll explain the difference between a democracy and a republic later).

Also, the Constitution, as written without any amendments, if you read it carefully, by its very vagueness, favored the elite, and resembled, by the checks and balances of power, the British system, born out of *common law*, of a Parliament, a Judicial system, and the Monarchy, with the Parliament having the most power... However, it lacked safeguards that would protect the common man. Therefore, during the Constitutional convention, the first *ten amendments* were added to the original document before certain states would *ratify* (agree upon) the Constitution, a move that *gave the common man equal rights and protections to those in the elite*, and it did indeed make all men equal; well, all free men that is, as stated in the preamble. Women, and slaves were not included because of the times, but that of course changed later.

Conclusion

The Founding Fathers firmly believed that only ethical, logical men should be allowed to govern, as taken from Plato's **The Republic,** ***and they should not interject their own religious beliefs into the making and upholding of the rules for a functional society, much like the Roman and Greek governments they admired…***

CHAPTER 2: WHAT'S THE DIFFERENCE BETWEEN A DEMOCRACY AND A REPUBLIC?

"In respect of temperance, courage, magnificence, and every other virtue, should we not carefully distinguish between the true son and the bastard?"

Plato, *The Republic*, Book VII

The basics…

A Democracy…

Ideally, *pure, or direct, democracies* only work well at the local level, where there are a few voting *directly* on local policy. There is no need for any kind of representative to act as a middle man; When the numbers of people involved in the vote is small, you're standing right there! Why have a middle man?

Religious and moral *paradigms* (a particular viewpoint of an individual or faction) *have a greater influence at this level.*

The disadvantage is that a democracy, as strictly defined, does not, cannot, work well at a state or national level due to the *disparity* (differences) and *distances* from the central government of the smaller locales (districts). Not only that, a *national popular vote* (where the candidate who gets the most votes in the country wins) in a pure democracy is *biased* (favors a particular *paradigm*) toward areas with larger populations…

So, the less populated areas will always be knocked out of the way of the larger, more populated areas… Not fair to the little guys way out in the sticks…

*Therefore our government, our nation, is not, cannot be, a **pure or direct** democracy.*

A Republic…

Republics, on the other hand, really only work well at the state or national level, where it is more convenient to have representatives from the locales taking the wishes of those he or she represents to the *sessions* (meetings) of the *legislature* (the part of our government that makes the laws). Hence the Founding Fathers, because of their classical training, saw the need for a council of elders (wise men chosen – elected -- from the educated elite, a.k.a. *the Senate,* and from the common people a.k.a. *the House of Representatives*) and an *Electoral College* (educated men who represent their locales for the purpose of voting for a presiding elder – a.k.a. the President)…

Because each state gets two representatives in the Senate despite their populations, the *Senate* is an *equalizer* for the states: Each state gets the same number of votes in the council as every other state, despite how populated each state is. Even a state with a low population gets an equal vote as states with larger populations. This system is also used at the state level. Each state has its own senate as well, their senators elected by the *districts* within the state.

We also have the *House of Representatives* that give voice to precisely defined locales and to the common man, and the number of representatives is dependent on the population coming from districts within each state. This gives a more direct influence of the populations within each district. Representatives do not need to come from the elite of society, and typically they do, indeed, represent the common man (it is much easier and cheaper to run for a seat in the House than it is in the Senate). The ancient republics did not have a House of Representatives.

In this modern concept of a republic, theoretically anyway, the law, the Constitution (by the way, the Romans and the Greeks also had constitutions), has enough "wiggle room" to make it flexible for the ebb and flow of *paradigms* within our society. How in the heck does it do that, given so many districts and so many people with so many different views of approaching particular problems?

The answer is, of all things, a *compromise between the two*: ***We are a republic and a democra*cy**! Crazy, huh? In modern political science jargon, our government is what is called a ***pluralistic democracy***...

Here's how a *pluralistic democracy* works: We, as individuals, vote for and through our representatives (a republic), basically because we don't have the time to worry about policy and policy making, nor do we have the time and money to drive all the way to the Capital. It's not like we're giving up our rights or our power as citizens to these representatives: We still have power in our government through not only the electoral process, but *we also have recourse in the courts.*

Hence, in comes another branch of our government, the *Judicial* branch. They are not law makers (well, until recently, that is), but the *enforcers* of the laws the legislative branch created. They also decide on the constitutionality of laws. So, in our modern government's case, an *individual can actually change a law* if it is found to be unconstitutional. Power to the people! Right on!

Yeah, well, there's more to it than that, but let's leave that for later (there are cheaters out there)…

And between these two branches, the legislative and the judicial, there is a third branch, the presiding, or administrative branch, a.k.a. the *Executive* branch. The individual who presides over the workings of the government is called… The King… Just kidding… No, he/she is called *the President* (actually, we almost had a king, believe it or not, and our first king would have been George Washington!). The President *presides* over the operation of the government, kind of like a CEO of a corporation. The president is elected by the Electoral College based on the votes from the various locales across the country.

This is true not only at the federal level, but also at the state level. Most state governments are modeled in much the same way as the federal government is modeled, complete with a governor, a senate, a house of representatives, and a state court system. State constitutions tend to be more lengthy and specific than the Federal Constitution.

Conclusion

The new government was designed to operate effectively at the national level, hence a republic, but gave individual citizens recourse through the Judicial system to challenge laws that may not be constitutional, *id est*, any law that may interfere with their individual rights, hence a democracy. The government designed by the Founding Fathers was, instead, a compromise of sorts: It was, as defined by modern political scientists, a *pluralistic democracy*, such that it was more a government by, and for, the people.

CHAPTER 3: REPUBLICANS VS. DEMOCRATS

"We are all Republicans"

Thomas Jefferson in his *First Inaugural Address* 1801

We must argue. Arguing is essential to the development of good ideas, and the suppression of bad ideas. Without it we would be mere lemmings following some *demagogue* (Greek for a "tub thumper"… telling us what we want to hear to get to some end, usually to gain or use his position of power for his own ends). Think of the effect of Hitler or Stalin on those past governments and how they suppressed opposing views – they "simply" imprisoned or killed their opposition… Pretty tough to argue with someone if we know they're going to throw us in prison or worse.

We, as a nation, without the ability to argue from our *paradigm*, could fall over the edge of a political and social *precipice* (like the edge of a cliff, only this cliff is an idea). The "Tub Thumpers" are many, and they are banging their tubs much more loudly these days, and in places where there did not used to be places… YouTube, Facebook, Twitter, etc… and they are thumping the tune that they think you want to hear…

Let's not be lemmings please: *Arguing is essentially a good thing*, as long as it's not violent; hence the need for political parties, at least until recently (George Washington warned us about factions, and recent events are playing out his warning). In our government, we've ended up with two main parties, the *Democrats* and the *Republicans*. There are other parties, in particular the Libertarians, and the Social Democrats, though those parties presently have a relatively small following, with Libertarians representing the largest of the smaller parties, about 10% of the population; but both parties are growing. The Socialist Party and The Communist Party once popular lost favor in this country after World War II, and are now essentially non-existent.

However, the chasm between the "right" and the "left" seems to have widened significantly within the last two decades, and thereby each seem less tolerant to opposing views… and this is a very dangerous place to be… because of the greater chasm between the two sides, the arguing could turn into "fisticuffs"… Actually, recent incidents prove our political discourse has turned violent. Look at what happened in Charlotte, Virginia, in 2017 between protesters and white supremacists.

To define what it means to be a Republican, we must take a look at the origins of the Parties. On the surface, you might think the two have opposing *paradigms:* You might think that the Democrats believe in a "democracy", where the people directly decide the policy. You might also think the Republicans, on the other hand, believe in a "republic", where the people are represented by an elite, *id est,* the *elected officials* who just happen to be members of the elite in society (remember Plato and the founding fathers?)…

Hm, well, not quite right…

Actually, the Democrats and the Republicans, as we know them, are both **republican** *parties* in theory. So, really, there isn't so much an opposing difference in the *how each views the* ***process*** *of our government…* ***both agree in electing officials to represent the locales.*** **Both parties believe in a** ***republican*** **process… in essence,** ***both parties are republican parties***.

First let me give some definitions. Bear with me…

Semantics is a concept that involves the intent and meaning of language, and implies that there are ways to manipulate language to fit an individual's *paradigm* within any given argument: A paradigm is a belief, or viewpoint, based on a particular *bias*… How words are structured within a sentence or statement to favor a certain point of view is an example of semantics. If you change the words, or the order of the words presented, or by adding or removing commas, *et cetera*, within a sentence, then it's meaning changes.

For example: My paradigm, in this book, is that I see the Republican Party has changed, and that this country in trouble. Someone else may think what is going on now is the best thing that ever happened to us. That individual has an opposing paradigm to mine. When we communicate our ideas, we, because of our bias, *use differing nuances within our language to favor our paradigm*; *id est (Latin for "that is")*, there are *semantic differences in our presentations* that create opposition within those who listen to us.

Another way to say this is we use forms of *propaganda* to promote our viewpoint within an argument. Typically this involves leaving out important information as much as telling non-truths.

If we disagree and cannot find any middle ground that is called a *semantic precipice*, also known as an *impasse*. An impasse is where no common ground can be found.

This has the potential to be dangerous… If there is an impasse, we could end up with people fighting and perhaps some people getting hurt: Think of the Civil War. But our system of government has the mechanism built into the Constitution that *should* take care of that problem, so long as people follow the Constitution as it is written…

Political Parties are groups of people that share a particular paradigm on how the government should deal with the particulars of running a country, *e.g.* such as taxes, and on what laws should be made or be taken off the books.

When we hold elections, we accept, as *per* the Constitution, that the winning party gets to impose *their* paradigm for the period of their service, and if we don't like it, we have the opportunity to elect them out for the next round. *Elections are great ways to settle impasses* (so long as there is no cheating… more on that later).

By agreement (again, the Constitution – remember the Founding Fathers were some pretty smart fellas), we are willing (perhaps grudgingly) to accept the opposing party's viewpoint for the next few years, and then, in the next election, we get another shot at imposing our paradigm. At least that's the way it's supposed to work. It's actually a bit more complicated than that (consider "infighting" between the Republicans and the

Democrats in both the House and the Senate, often coming to stalemates)…

But… and here's the catch… the opposition between parties, Republicans and Democrats, has nothing to do with how locales are represented; everyone agrees on that… *The opposition of parties lay within in the vagueness of the Constitution:* How each Party *interprets* the Constitution based on their particular paradigm can lead to struggles within the legislature and between the branches of government as well. These struggles may also mirror the differences of opinions within and between local districts.

The origins and the differences between Democrats and Republicans...

The origin of the Democratic Party...

The Democratic Party had its unofficial beginnings in the 1828 Presidential campaign, when John Quincy Adams, a *National Republican* (not the same as the modern Republican Party) candidate elected President in 1824, was accused of being corrupt and of being a *Federalist* and a *Whig* (those who believed in a strict, literal, interpretation of the Constitution and a strong central government). It was perceived at the time that the government had become, in its very short life so far, very corrupt (as positions of power tend to attract those who have selfish motives), and a government by, and for, the elite. The common people were looking for a savior... Enter *Andrew Jackson*, a war hero and a man of low beginnings, a common man...

The Democratic Party, which grew out of the *Jeffersonian Democratic-Republican Party*, was founded by Andrew Jackson and Martin Van Burin after that 1828 election, where Jackson won, and was propelled by those who wanted less centralized government and less interference from the central government. It was also, informally, called the *Jacksonian Party*.

The Democratic Party was a party that claimed to be the party of the common man, and it was very anti-central banks. *Alliis in verbis (Latin for "in other words"), they wanted more power at the local level, among the common man, where they made their own local decisions; a democracy-like paradigm – hence "Democrats".*

The Democratic Party was the dominant party for the next twenty plus years, until just before the Civil War, and it was this period of time where the elite got their come-upends, and our government seemed to have "found itself"; it became more a government of the people, not of the elite, and *preferred a strong Executive branch* that could have more control over the more elite Legislative and Judicial branches, strengthening, and giving more flexibility, to the "checks and balances" aspect of the Constitution.

Jackson, ironically, eventually moved to form a stronger Federal government to combat the encroaching push from States rights proponents, a move that opposed the beliefs of the Democratic Party, causing Southern states to push for secession from the Federation, the United States, and would have profound effects eventually contributing to the Civil War. This contributed to the change *These* United States before the war, to *The* United States after the war. It was also the beginning of the rise of a stronger Executive branch, a trend that continues today.

The Democratic Party at that time was *pro-slavery*, and was the *favored party of the slave-owning Southern states*. After the Civil War, the party fell out of favor for several decades, mainly because of its *pro-white beliefs* and the defeat of the Southern, Democratic (Confederate) states.

That is, until Woodrow Wilson won the Presidency under the Democratic ticket in 1912, who then was in office for two terms and then again in the 1930's when FDR was elected, who was in office for three terms. These wins were due mostly to economics, where there was a recession in the late 1890's and early 1900's, and then later the Great Depression in the late 1920's and early 1930's. Much of the blame for those recessions fell on the Republican Administrations who were in office at the time the recessions occurred. The mechanics of how that happened are complex, much having to do with the faulty theories of economics at the time, and the Republican administrations believing in those theories.

Also, just as important, somewhat because of the recessions, there was a good deal of unrest from within the working class people because of working conditions and low wages. The *Unions* gained power and influence, pushing people toward the Democratic Party who decried itself the "Party of the Working Class". It was also during this time that the *Socialist* and *Communist* Parties gained footing within our political system: Both parties were popular among the working class, where each reached their greatest followings during the period between 1900 to the early 1950's.

The "Flip": The Democratic Party remained the dominant party in the Southern states until the mid-1960's when the *Equal Rights Amendment* was introduced, signed into law by Lyndon B. Johnson, a Democratic President, and a Democratically dominated Congress... ***This flip from being pro-white to pro-civil rights drove many in the Southern states to switch to the Republican Party, and many in the Republican Party to switch to the Democratic Party in the Northern states!***

The Democratic Party also flipped in other regards, favoring more central government involvement in regulations because of corruption from large banks and large corporations, as well as environmental and resource issues within our boarders…

The origins of the Republican Party…

The Republican Party emerged and was founded in 1854 for the *primary purpose of stopping new Western states being allowed to decide whether they would be slave states or not, and eliminating slavery founded by abolitionist* Hannibal Hamlin, pressing Abraham Lincoln as its Presidential candidate. Lincoln was chosen, among other reasons, because of his "low" beginnings, attracting many who previously followed the Jacksonian governments, weakening the Democratic vote in the North. Many of that first party also wanted the black man to have equal voting rights (suffrage) to the white man. It was the favored party in the Northern states because of the strong abolitionist sentiments (the Missouri Compromise essentially put the Northern States and the Southern States in conflict, where slavery was illegal in the Northern States and not in the Southern States, but the new Western States needed direction on whether slavery would be legal there… Hence, the beginnings of the Civil War). ***The Northern states were also where most of the nation's industries and most of the large banks were located, which made the Republican Party the party favored by businesses and banks.*** Needless to say the Republican Party was pivotal in the events that led up to the Civil War.

Ironically, the man who replaced Lincoln after Lincoln was assassinated in April of 1865 was a Democrat from the Southern state of Tennessee, Andrew Johnson, and who had the support of the Republican Party because of his stance on punishment of the Southern States after the war. It was the Republicans that pushed the Thirteenth Amendment through and the proclamation of freedom to the former slaves. ***The Republican Party, the party that caused the collapse of slavery, was also the Party favored by businesses and opposed Unions and "socialist" ideas.***

The Republican Party has, then, essentially maintained dominance within the U.S. government, with the exceptions of only a few, albeit very important, periods, within our government since the Civil War.

The parties as they are now... A movement toward extremism...

The Republican Party has, for reasons I'll explain in the next chapter, linked itself to the much more radical right.

The Republican Party has evolved now to a party that focuses on less taxes (favors big business) and less spending (conservative economics); an evolution that can mark its beginning in the elections of 1912. However these concepts have reached within the last four decades an all-time extreme: *Very* low taxes, especially for the upper 1%, the uber-rich, which is too low to maintain a workable government, causing an increase in national debt.

As much as the Republican Party loves him, Ronald Reagan has left us with an untenable legacy of too low taxes for the big businesses without any significant cut in spending (Trickle Down Economics, aka "Voodoo" or *Reaganomics*: Take less money from the businesses and they will lower prices and pay their workers more... didn't happen... they took the money and put it back into their own pockets). Along with that is another danger to this new attitude among Republican lawmakers: Use public trust funds to finance their low taxes...

...This is a dangerous precedent: We should learn from what happened in Argentina, our greatest competitors in the world until their collapse in 2001 (see the reference for *False Economy* by Allan Beattie in the bibliography)...

The Republican Party also, most recently, seems to have moved toward a more extreme pro-white and pro-religion paradigm, much like the original Democratic Party, though recently much of the propaganda coming from the conservative right is including people of different races and ethnicity (CRTV as an example).

Within the last decade the *Federalists* and *Libertarians* have also been inching their way into the political scene via the Republican Party. The *Federalists* believe in a pure interpretation of the Constitution where grey and shadowy areas such as the rights of women to have abortions or the right of people of non-heterosexual orientations to enter into marriage have no place in the political arena, and should not be included in the protections listed in the Constitution. The *Libertarians,* and in particular *The Tea Party,* believe in absolutely the least amount of government possible, and still have a workable government with individuals holding all rights within "common law". Some would even want to eliminate government all together and go completely to common law. Not a good idea, as was demonstrated in Britain following the Magna Carta, and certainly not a Republican concept.

The Democratic Party has evolved into something else, far more left, as well; it now favors rights for *all* individuals, including equality for those outside of what might be considered "the norm", equality for non-citizens, and it emphasizes more government help to those who are lesser in our society, no longer just the party of the common, working man… a socialist concept; and yet even another irony, it was the Democrats who, under Lyndon B. Johnson, introduced the Equal Rights Amendment (this is the party that originally wanted states, especially the new Western states at that time, to decide whether they would have slaves or not). The Democratic Party has recently lost followers, especially during the last election, due to inner-Party politics, too many paradigms within the Party, and "crony-ism".

And now, it seems, from the ashes of the Democratic Party's melt-down of the 2016 elections arises the new Phoenix, the *Social Democratic Party*.

Conclusion

The extremes we are seeing lately are the result of complex mechanisms that can be boiled down to unhappiness within disenfranchised groups of people, believing they have lost any say or power within our government and members of the uber-rich and extreme factions taking advantage of that disillusionment. But the reality, complex or not, is these extreme paradigms are taking hold and moving into our government. The fix is not with the groups or with the people in general. The fix is entirely somewhere else…

CHAPTER 4: WIN AT ANY COST!

"The truly scary thing about undiscovered lies is that they have a greater capacity to diminish us than exposed ones. They erode our strength, our self-esteem, our very foundation."

Cheryl Hughes , from *Race, Social Identity, and Human Dignity* Social Philosophy Today Vol. 16

If you are about my age, approaching 70 years, you'll likely remember the overall feeling of dissatisfaction the general populace had with the government starting from about 1964 with Lyndon Johnson's Presidency up until the end of Ronald Reagan's Presidency in the late 1980's. It was almost a joke, the proverbial $50,000 hammer, and the $20,000 toilet seat (gross exaggerations, of course, but a common perception among the populace at the time). It would have been funny (lots of cartoons were in the newspapers in those days about this "joke") except there really was a kind of "fleecing of America" (and still is), and blatantly so, it seems. On top of this was rising inflation. It didn't matter whether it was the Republicans or Democrats in office. Neither Party really seemed to be running the show. It was more like some unseen puppet master was behind the scenes directing the drama.

There was a strong sense of corruption being within our government, but also a sense of helplessness. So what's a normal everyday kind a' guy or gal to do? You vote one government in and it's just as bad as the previous government, except maybe with a little different "flavor". There didn't seem to be much change with each election. This was frustrating for the public, to say the least; a formula for apathy, culminating in the 1970's.

Though most US citizens at the time were relatively stoic, and they still believed in America and the American Dream, people were "pissed off": Inflation was a problem, among other things, and when you mess with people's money, they become unhappy. With inflation rates in the double digits, their money having less value and barely able to put food on the table, paying taxes just seemed to make it worse; especially if you saw waste and corruption in the State and Federal governments. We were still pouring money into ineffective "anti-communist" programs, and the cold war was smoldering all the while under our feet.

1964… Vietnam, though not the first, was a big indicator of corruption: The veil covering the underlying motive of such an untenable and unwinnable war was thin; those who were there (only about a third of those going to Vietnam were actually involved in combat… most were in support roles, where those behind the lines could see the corruption) coming back with stories of waste and corruption beyond anything we've seen in the past. *Worse, it was all on the evening news every night.*

The CIA was playing dirty tricks on the Central American countries in the 1960's, in the name of stopping communism, but in actuality not because of communism, but because of fruit and rubber trees. Heaven forbid a country become Nationalistic and have the desire to run their own countries, controlling their own resources.

And on and on… Nixon and Watergate, Reagan and the Iran-Contra affair, all were part of the same problem: The overall feeling and view was that our government was corrupt, pure and simple.

What happened to the Republican Party?

They started out on a very moral precept: End slavery. Good. Got it done…

Once done, what's next? Punish the Southern States, that's what. Check (my great grandfather fought in the Confederate Army, and after the war, because of his affiliation, lost the family farm somehow, then had to move West and, ironically, bought really bad farm land in Missouri from the US Government)… Done, sort of: The Republicans didn't get exactly what they wanted; Lincoln and then his successor, Johnson, "Let 'em up slowly", where the hard-liner Republicans wanted the South to feel real pain for their transgressions. There is still resentment in the South because of this attitude, and a lot of people are still flying the Confederate flag because of it; and *worse, and most confounding, they associate conservatism and the Republican Party now with the old Confederate ideals.*

(This flip within the constituency of the Republican Party is dripping with the juice of irony: If people would read some good scholarly books on the South and economics, such as *False Economy* by Allen Beattie, they would understand what the Confederacy actually represented, especially economically, and it is very likely they would choose not fly the Confederate flag).

...And the Republican Party used that win against the South as a board to sail on for the next forty plus years, dominating the political scene until Woodrow Wilson won the Presidency, and during that forty years after the Civil War followed an already established imperialistic program ousting the Spanish out of the Philippines and Cuba.

The election of 1912 was a pivotal year for the Republican Party. Howard Taft, the incumbent president, elected in 1908 when Roosevelt refused the nomination, was considered a "progressive" Republican who pushed Tariff reforms and the formation of the Income Tax. The measures passed, but many citizens and congressmen were angered by this push, which caused a split in the Republican Party into two factions, the "Insurgents" and the "Progressives". This was the first year where the Republican Party, the insurgents, became "fiscally conservative" where here-to-fore they had been in favor of higher taxes and fairer tariffs. The Democrats, in part because of this split, won the election.

We "found our muscles" so to speak, and from our lessons learned from the Civil War, realized our industrial strength and our vast resources just under our feet. We learned we could "kick behinds" and the world in general was watching as the "Great Giant" awakened; eventually showing all our muscles in World War II, and placing us as number one country in the world. *Our industries also well learned the profit of war.* It was hard for us to let go of that little golden goose: War and more war meant more profits.

It is important to know that we were warned about the banks and corporations leveling their power of influence within our government, and they have done so, using both Parties to do so; although the Republican Party seems to have become the favored son.

The Republican attitude was also the same as the popular economic theory at the time: If we produced, produced, and produced, we could make even more money, which lead us into the Great Depression, and that got Herbert Hoover and the Republicans ousted from government and FDR was elected in.

Essentially, the Republican Party got a big head. They got greedy. Beginning in 1912, they lost their original purpose and sided with those who had to gain from an unfettered market: The Big Corporations and the Big Banks… eventually taking on an economic philosophy similar to that found in two novels, ironically, of fiction: Ayn Rand's *The Fountainhead* (1943) and *Atlas Shrugged* (1957).

After Truman and the Korean War, it became back and forth jousts between the Democrats and the Republicans. The Republicans just didn't have enough oomph to win all the elections like they used to. The old ways just weren't working. *They had to do something…*

…and with a little help from a couple of billionaire brothers in the early 1990's…

When in doubt, consult a consultant, especially one who is a "believer". Beginning in the 1990's, after Bill Clinton won the

Presidency, and the Democrats controlled both the Senate and the House (remember Lyndon Johnson's administration also had a dominant Democratic Senate and House) *Republicans panicked.*

It seemed unthinkable, since Jimmy Carter won the Presidency in 1976, that another Democrat had won the Presidency, and worse, they had lost the Senate and House as well… ***Enter savior Grover Norquist*** and his Wednesday lunches he held for Republican leaders and congressmen. Norquist began a series of discussions and planning sessions that would help the Republican Party win elections "at any cost". He proposed strategies that, at least from any reasonable person's perspective, essentially told the Republicans to "cheat"…

…One of his suggestions, not a new concept, but very effective if done all across the Nation, was *Gerrymandering*. You want to win? Win as many *local* elections as possible, and once you control the local areas, *move the district lines in such a way that some districts with more voters in the opposition lose population and others, the ones where you have more Republican, gain population* giving the Republicans more votes from the local districts: A dirty little trick, but one that has effectively helped the Republican Party regain the House of Representatives, and then later, the Presidency, and ultimately, the Senate.

…He also recommended more PR… Sell the Republican Party, use the media to your advantage. Use or create "talking heads" to espouse your dictum: People who are good salesmen, to talk and inject misinformation into the public's mind: *e.g.*, Rush Limbaugh started out as a disc jockey, with no background or training in politics, but very vocal politically, and was, is, a "believer".

...Control the media: If you can't get the mainstream media to swallow your line, then create a news media that spins your side better than the other side; so called "fair and balanced", and ultimately owning a large share of the media (only six large corporations own 90% of the media in the U.S.).

Control the media and you control the minds of the people...

Why control the media? Because... The President is the Party's representative in the Executive position. Control the Executive branch, push for increased power at the Executive level, and even with just controlling the House, you can dominate the government: Using the media you can convince the voters, *via* propaganda, to vote for your party line; then you can push laws that favor your paradigm. You can place judges in positions of determining the legality of policy that favor your supporters. Dominate the government, and you dominate policy, giving advantage to those who supported your candidates. This is not only power, folks, this is bordering on absolute power, and "Absolute power corrupts..."

...Use social media; as it has evolved now into a media that enters the public's mind at a very personal level, kind of like talking to an old friend who believes the same things that you do, even though your old friend might not be telling you the truth: *He is simply telling you things you want to hear, getting you stirred up and riled at things that otherwise would be trivial.*

Recently, with the introduction of digital voting machines, programing can be inserted to change the vote to favor a particular party, as was demonstrated by elections affected by voting machining program in the Florida Congressional elections.

…Also, *to gain more voters*, the Republican Party proselytized religion and religious leaders, banging the abortion drum, giving the Party a new abolition, turning people against the opposition based on "moral" means.

Remember what the Founding Fathers said about allowing religion into government? Not a good idea then and not a good idea now.

The Republicans, in another move to gain advantage, used the conservative dominated Supreme Court, via a law suit, to decide votes placed in the key state of Florida in the 2000 elections favored the Republican candidate, George W. Bush, giving him the Presidency.

…The Republican Party became bed partners with the super radicals: Once a "grass roots" movement, the Tea Party, having its beginnings with the Libertarian billionaire Koch brothers in the 1990's, now arguably represents the mainstream Republican Party more than it did as a sideline. By bringing them into the Party in 2009, after Barack Obama won the 2008 election, their votes, and support, was gained where otherwise votes would have been siphoned off the Republican votes and gave Republicans the advantage over the Democrats in Congressional elections, leading to a Republican dominated Congress. It was a logistical move, but as in any such decision, *there is a* **caveat**, *a price to be paid.*

…Worse, now it seems that our once great nemesis is manipulating the public's attitude and mindset, as they seem to be doing all over the world. The Russian government is still our enemy, just not the way you might think. They are spreading misinformation through the use of social media, and our own right wing media isn't helping. The "talking heads" pick up their misinformation and tell it like it's the absolute truth. For some odd reason (perhaps not so odd), Russia wants the Republicans (what might be better called the "new" Republican Party) to keep control of the US government. This should concern and frighten all of us. I remember the Cold War, and this feels much the same, only more insidious.

This is not to say the Democrats aren't guilty of similar actions (the banks and corporations contribute money to both sides of the aisle, corrupting both), but we're not talking about them right now…

We have been fooled into thinking we must win at any cost…

Why? Because being a major player in politics means money and it means power. Neither party can afford to lose power… too many hands in the till, too much power to be had by those supporters operating behind the scenes.

This is a slippery slope. Once started, it is no easy thing to stop. The Republican Party, because of this new need to win, has factionalized and moved to extremes. Extremes are bad for anyone and any government…

Conclusion

Ok, so, where are we now? Look, here's what's happened in a nutshell: By using time-tested and unsavory means of political manipulation (Gerrymandering), propaganda (talking heads, conservative media), playing on people's religious sensitivities, and decrying patriotism, the Republican Party has, in effect, created a disparate chasm between members of society, this from a once honorable purpose: To be the saviors of the slaves.

What is wrong with the Republican Party today is the Republican Party wants to win elections, and win them at any cost, ethics "be damned"; starting with the 1970 elections with Nixon and Watergate, and continue to this day…

…The Republican Party has sold its soul to the proverbial devil… The extremists: The extreme conservative and religious factions who until recently held only a token representation; the same kind of conservatism my father feared in the early 1960's from the John Birch Society.

CHAPTER 5: HOW TO FIX OUR POLITICAL SYSTEM

"The people always have some champion whom they set over themselves and nurse into greatness."

Plato, *The Republic*, Book II

Besides Lincoln, I think the best President the Republican Party ever had in office was Teddy Roosevelt. He was an imperialist, no doubt, but those were the times, but he truly loved this Country and its people. He established National Parks to protect that very rare resource in the world: Wilderness and natural resources. *He stood up to the Big Banks and Corporations*. He believed that banks and business were important, but not so much so that the people took second chair, nor to have them control our government. He was not the workers friend, and was very anti-union, but he helped establish *regulations* that made sure our products, our food, and our savings were safe. He instilled in the American People a trust and confidence that has not been matched until his nephew, Franklin D. Roosevelt became President. Teddy Roosevelt and his nephew were *ethical* men; perhaps not moral from many people's perspective, *but they believed in fair play*.

I make this point about Roosevelt because he represents the one most outstanding characteristic our Founding Fathers wanted in a leader: To approach the position of leadership in an *ethical* stance. Note that I do not include "moral" in this description.

Ethics is where ***one engages in fair play regardless of one's moral paradigm***. We teach our children to play fair on the playing field. We want to win the meet, but not through cheating. Better to lose than to cheat; no one likes a cheater. This does not mean that the candidate ignore his or her religious beliefs; it simply means that *fair play, within the government, takes precedence over any moral belief.*

If there is any quote appropriate to this idea it is, most naturally, the Golden Rule: *"Do unto others as you would have them do unto you."*

Problems with our political system… We need to understand this in order to fix the system…

Fixing a disjointed political system is no easy task. Poli-Sci 101 teaches us that *positions in government*, even a lowly local position, *gives its holder some level of power and recognition*, and *power tends to attract certain types of people who seek not the position itself, but the power and recognition that position offers them.* ***By its very nature, government has a built in recipe for corruption.***

I once attended a Republican gathering in St. Louis, Missouri in the mid 1980's. While there, one of the young candidates for an upcoming election was campaigning while people came in. One of the older, and very distinguished looking, members came up to him, and like a father guiding a child, quietly told him that this was not the place, and with his hand on the young man's back led him away from the doorway. That moment was an epiphany for me, causing me to realize just how carefully *the candidates are trained to participate in very a complex political process.*

A political party looks for and grooms people they think will have the greatest chances of winning political contests from the very beginning of their political careers, very often starting with local school boards where politics can be "in your face"; this teaches the up and coming candidates the art of campaigning, and, if they win, to deal with political pressure and criticism from the most vocal of all citizens: Parents.

This grooming process is scripted by the party leaders and officials who have ties with those *with money* needed to push the candidates up the political ladder. So very often than not, *those with money* are either from "big business" or are corporations themselves, and are also those who have much to gain when certain legislation or regulation is up for consideration: Hence, as it stands now, *corporations and the uber-rich, then, are the ones who are actually, by providing funds for candidates' campaigns, choosing the candidates beholding to them,* directly or indirectly, through surreptitious means; using propaganda and misinformation, fooling people into believing their choices of candidates are the best choices even though those same said candidates, in their decisions on such matters, *favor not the people who voted them in but the corporations and the rich who paid for their campaigns.*

Worse, some individuals are placed in candidate positions by corporations through the political party with the very intent of passing laws or regulations that favor that corporation's interest; or, the candidate is placed in such a position to appoint people with the corporation's interest at heart to important positions that dictate regulation once he or she is elected, ignoring the needs of the very people who elected them. A great part of the problem, then, lies within this interference by "special interests".

George Washington warned us against factions in his parting address. Political parties, and the micro-interest groups within each, are, in fact, factions, and factions are by nature self-serving. The more at stake politically and financially, the greater the dishonesty and manipulation in the struggle to obtain positions of power. A candidate is merely the representative of the political party's, and the sponsoring backer's, interests. *If candidates can be removed from being obliged to these interests, we stand some chance of having the kind of leader our Founding Fathers, and Plato, imagined.*

Our government is no longer or necessarily by the people or for the people: It seems, more and more, it is for the rich and the corporations. Alexander Hamilton, and other Founding Fathers, foresaw this, and Teddy Roosevelt is probably rolling in his grave right now.

The problem now is that campaigning is so expensive, and so many media options where voters get their information of the candidates. The present system is overwhelmed by misleading media not only from television, newspapers and radio, but also, and perhaps even more so, from social media. So many choices means an individual can pick and choose those media that appeal to their own belief system: People hear what they want to hear, and the media is very good at giving it to them.

Worse, digital media has algorithms that find exactly what people are looking at and searching for and what and where their interests lay; *they can fine tune their* ***propaganda*** *to lead someone down a self-gratifying path, feeding them what they want to hear with the intent of getting them to vote for their candidate.*

Other problems with our political system…

It could be argued that the greatest problem that now exists in our political machine is the *digital voting machine.* A recent hacker's convention in Los Vegas invited youth, children as young as five years old, to try to hack into voting machines; the same machines used at the polls: One child, a twelve year old girl, hacked into one of the machines they had set up for that purpose in seventeen minutes. Even worse, a young man, Clinton Curtis, who wrote software for the voting machines testified in 2010 to writing in computer script at the request of Rep. Tom Finney, speaker of the Florida House, that would favor the Republican Party in the vote in South Florida during the 2004 elections. Digital voting machines are dangerous, and contain natural holes for interference and manipulation.

Also, our former nemesis, Russia, as well as other countries including China, has become an expert at digital interference at all levels, local, state, and federal, using social media to control the public's opinion of opposing sides. I believe the FBI and the intelligence community is working very hard in neutralizing this very real threat to our political system, *but the best defense is the voters themselves recognizing the manipulations,* using methods described Edward Filene's publication "The Seven Devices of Propaganda", which is reproduced in the Appendix.

Many states now have both the voting machines and a backup paper ballot. The paper ballots can be made so that there is no doubt as to who the voter was voting for during the counting process. In Missouri, the ballots are like the old "ScanTron" sheets, where dark pens are used to blacken in a vertical "dash" that can be read by a special machine just for that purpose. The dashes are far enough apart so there is no doubt of who the voter was voting for. The voter fills in the dashes, and then places his or her ballot into the reader which then electronically reads the dashes. The electronic reader counts votes and gives an initial win for a candidate, but the paper ballot is the official ballot, not the digital readout, and recounts would be, should be, done without requests by any candidate, done by hand, reading the paper ballots. The hand-read count would be the official result.

A Vetting Process for candidates…

I spent a good deal of time reading through volumes of internet posts and sites on how to "fix" our political system. They ranged from reasonable to silly and whacky, from intelligent to outright dangerous. Some want the political system to be completely online, where every mobile device gets a vote, while others wish to return to paper and "warm-bloods", people who interview the candidates personally, one on one, much like a senate hearing, with no digital input at all. The former is nothing more than equation for pure interference and hacking, while the latter is slow and cumbersome. There are even those who wish to throw out the Constitution, or re-write it to fit the modern environment: Our Constitution is just fine, thank you very much; leave it alone.

Also, if you want to keep other religions from taking over our government, keep your religion out, too. *When you discriminate against a particular religion, race, or creed, those factions react by becoming more active in government.* Let's not forget why the Founding Fathers wanted to keep religion out of government in the first place.

We begin fixing the political system during the *pre-election* period, the time of choosing candidates and campaigning, so that undesirable (corrupt, incompetent, self-serving, etc.) individuals cannot dominate the political scene; what is called a *vetting* process and the removal from our political system the factors that damage the process itself.

Our first task, then, is to find a way to vet individuals who seek positions in government. As it is now, the vetting process is called *the primaries*. It has been argued that the primaries are even more important that the main election, because it is there we chose who gets to run for the main offices. The Party helps choose those who it thinks will best represent the Party, but during the primaries the voters then choose among them; once a person is chosen, only he or she may run for election. *That is why the Party system is so important to the electoral process. A corrupt Party, however, gives us a corrupt election.* There needs to be a vetting algorithm that bypasses the crony-ism and private interest interference, even, perhaps, at the expense of bypassing or eliminating political parties all together.

Besides vetting candidates, there should also be laws to prevent cheating once a dominant party gains positions of power. The first on the list of laws should be making Gerrymandering illegal…

A "fix" for our political system…

Once upon a time, newspapers would invite the candidates to submit answers to important questions, questions that provided the voters with some semblance of what each candidate stood for. It has been proposed a return to something like the written word for candidate selection, making sure all sides are represented, not the side the media wishes to promote. But with television and digital media it would be a relatively simple task to establish a similar "vetting" process, except instead of the candidates responding to questions from the newspaper, ***certain chosen individuals within our society,*** **delegates**, preferably people well-educated and well versed in the political process ask questions of candidates. The questions would be designed to ferret out lies and ulterior goals of the candidate. These interviews would be televised on public television stations that could be re-broadcast on internet and print outlets, paid for by the government, hence by the taxpayers themselves, *which cuts out the obligations to financial backers and places the obligations back to the voters.*

To establish the vetting process, there needs to be a set of *guidelines*, available to the public, to describe the characteristics that would expose propaganda and the undesirables. The guidelines should be presented to the public in all venues well before the campaigns begin; *alliis in verbis*, every form of media where people gather their information and make decisions, such as TV news, radio news, newspapers, online media, social media, etc. *These guidelines should be developed by ethical people well educated in the political process:* Perhaps including Professors of Political Science, Professors of Constitutional Law, Historians, and Journalist recognized for their neutral stance and intelligence (the elite as Plato imagined them, not the uber-rich).

The guidelines should include methods to recognize factors that damage the political process and opinions of voters. The guidelines should give the voter the tools needed to make intelligent decisions without influence or bias toward one party or the other. These guidelines should be applied to all candidates by the voting public, and all voters should be, at the very least, aware of their existence, and perhaps even expected to know these guidelines.

A final thought: It wouldn't hurt to return to teaching Civics in our schools; it is essential to citizenship in this country for young people to be well versed in the political process. I mean this as a separate course from American Government and American History. To teach our children not only the responsibilities of citizenship, but also how to detect insincerity and ulterior motives should be an essential skill young people, and all voters, should learn.

Conclusion:

The "fix" is in changing the campaign laws so that our government officials are placed in positions of power without the interference of special interests, the rich and big business; using public funds instead of private funds to fund the dissemination of political rhetoric, and the laws should be written in such a way to encourage ethics and fair play between the candidates before the elections occur, which would also include rules for political adds. After the elections, laws need to be made that prevent "cheating" by the incoming government that favor their winning elections in the future, such as Gerrymandering and voter identification manipulations. There also need to be laws at the Federal level that standardize the way states collect and count votes, giving "hard" paper, ballots preference over "soft" digital ballots.

CHAPTER 6: A REPUBLICAN'S CREDO

"When a people agree to form themselves into a republic (they) mutually resolve and pledge themselves to each other, rich and poor alike, to support this rule of equal justice among them....A republic, properly understood, is a sovereignty of justice, in contradistinction to a sovereignty of will."

Thomas Paine, in a pamphlet *Common Sense*, January 10, 1776

While reading this, think of *Abraham Lincoln* and *Teddy Roosevelt*, the truly great Republican Presidents…

…I think of my parents…

A Republican…

A Republican is, then, someone who *values what the Founding Fathers valued*: A government that *represents the people*, not itself, not only with regard to their wishes, but to their needs, and it does this using a balance of powers and enlistments of "helpers" as defined in the Constitution.

A Republican, as defined by Plato, *does not cheat to gain power.* A Republican, if they should lose an election, gracefully bows to the winning side and does not try to interfere with their agenda, remembering the people elect those who rise to the position of leadership. A Republican understands their turn will come, as *all things follow cycles*.

A Republican, as defined by Plato, *is ethical*: they do not rely on lying, misinformation, or propaganda; in other words, a Republican relies on *fair play*. A Republican must always be above those who would compromise ethics for power.

A Republican *does not follow the dogma of despots*, but rather listens to all ideas with *discernment*, and makes political judgement based on the ideals and spirit of what is good for all, not just the few of the uber-rich or extremists who would wish themselves to control our society.

A Republican *does not allow religion into, or to dominate, our government*. They may or may not be religious and are tolerant of other people's beliefs, but they believe the government's function is, using ethical means, to act as a conduit to tend to of the needs of the nation as a whole, operating within the confines laid out in the structure of the Constitution.

A Republican believes, as defined in the Constitution, in *regulated manufacture, service and trade* to insure an adequate infrastructure, safe products, a clean environment, and trade fair to all. A Republican believes in a *Trust* of participants in trade, and endeavors to apply and force anti-trust laws to keep trade and commerce fair.

A Republican believes in the *use of essential, fair, and progressive taxes* to provide basic essentials to the people: Essentials such as a militia, a system of public protection (fire departments, police departments, health departments, transport, etc.).

A Republican believes in the *betterment of the people* in order to raise among their youth future, ethical leaders, wise and enterprising business people, and teachers to teach the youth to take our places in our future.

A Republican believes in the *protection of the resources* possessed by this United States; resources that include not only minerals, air, water, and natural reserves, but also among the people themselves.

A Republican believes in the *sanctity* of Public Trusts Funds, insuring a safe and comfortable twilight of age for all citizens.

A Republican does not believe in *little* or *no* government where a common, unfettered, law is the rule.

A Republican *believes in the rights of individuals* as defined in the Constitution, and *does not discriminate* with regard to race, color, or creed.

Conclusion

In short, to call yourself a Republican, you must follow the example of the first Republicans; **you must be one of the *elite*: the kind described by Plato and our Founding Fathers; you must stand above the selfish and self-serving and be known among all as a *protector* of the Constitution as**

laid out by our Founding Fathers, and of the citizens of The United States of America.

If you cannot abide by the above definitions, you should not call yourself a Republican; do not forget that the original purpose of the Republican Party was to free the slaves in the Southern States: As a Republican, you agree to a certain code of justice and equality, as defined in the Constitution…

As a Republican, you are to be an example to the world as a participant in the greatest political experiment in history: The Republic of the United States of America…

...And in the end, for all of us, a higher sense of calling...

"I believe order is better than chaos, creation better than destruction. I prefer gentleness to violence, forgiveness to vendetta. On the whole I think that knowledge is preferable to ignorance, and I am sure that human sympathy is more valuable than ideology."

Kenneth Clark, *Civilisation,* television series, BBC, 1969

APPENDIX

Recognizing Propaganda

Seven simple techniques to recognize propaganda written by Edward Filene and distributed as a pamphlet in 1939 by The Institute for Propaganda Analysis, and later expanded by Clyde Miller in 1941(these have since been much used and expanded; please see the Wikipedia reference on "Proganda Techniques")

The Seven Devices of Propaganda

Bandwagon: "Has as its theme 'everybody - at least all of us - is doing it!' and thereby tries to convince the members of a group that their peers are accepting the program and that we should all jump on the bandwagon rather than be left out." "Everybody is doing this." You've heard that before. The idea here is to convey the notion that if you don't get aboard you will be left out. This can also appear as news organizations jump on a "story" so as not to be left out.

Card Stacking: "Involves the selection and use of facts or falsehoods, illustrations or distractions, and logical or illogical statements to give the best or the worst possible case for an idea, program, person, or product." You might also include Cherry-Picking. The propagandist uses only those facts and details that support their argument. The selected reasons are used to support the conclusion. You will get misled if you do not notice that important details are missing. The worst part of card-stacking is that it can be very difficult to detect if you are not really knowledgeable about the subject.

Glittering Generalities: "Associating something with a 'virtue word' and creating acceptance and approval without examination of the evidence." These are vague, broad statements that will connect with the audience's beliefs and values. They really don't say anything substantive. Slogans make great examples. The vagueness means that the implications, though varying for different people, are always favorable. Think of peace, freedom, justice, family values, etc.

You can check if something is a glittering generality by asking questions of the speech/slogan such as "How?" or "With what?" or "By what means?" If those questions are unanswered, then you may be dealing with a glittering generality. If they do answer the questions, see if their answers are substantive (details supported by evidence) or whether their answers are even more glittering generalities.

Name-Calling: "Giving an idea a bad label and therefore rejecting and condemning it without examining the evidence." This is the use of negative words or labels to create prejudice against some person, group or idea. If you fall for this you have been driven to reach a conclusion *without* examining the evidence.

Plain Folks: "The method by which a speaker attempts to convince the audience that he or she and his or her ideas are good because they are 'of the people,' the 'plain folks.'" The person speaking will adopt a demeanor that makes them look like "everyman." They will appear to connect with the audience and their point of view. Careful choice of clothing, vocabulary, and mannerisms is necessary to make the identity connection. Hitler was quite good at this.

Testimonial: "Consists in having some respected or hated person say that a given idea or program or product is good or bad." This technique has a well-known someone endorse, recommend or approve of a product, cause or program. Pop celebrities can work well here. Remember that testimonials aren't worth much, particularly if the endorser is not an authority in the field.

Transfer: "Carries the respect and authority of something respected to something else to make the latter accepted. Also works with something that is disrespected to make the latter rejected." This is an effort to transfer your approval of something you respect and approve of to another something that the propagandist wants you to approve of. Using a flag as a background for photographs helps.

Edward Filene, 1939

A more complete quote from Alexander Hamilton's [Objections and Answers Respecting the Administration], [18 August 1792]

[This is taken from the complete text as found in the National Archives in the Library of Congress.]

"The truth unquestionably is, that the only path to a subversion of the republican system of the Country is, by flattering the prejudices of the people, and exciting their jealousies and apprehensions, to throw affairs into confusion, and bring on civil commotion. Tired at length of anarchy, or want of government, they may take shelter in the arms of monarchy for repose and security.

Those then, who resist a confirmation of public order, are the true Artificers of monarchy—not that this is the intention of the generality of them. Yet it would not be difficult to lay the finger upon some of their party who may justly be suspected. When a man unprincipled in private life desperate in his fortune, bold in his temper, possessed of considerable talents, having the advantage of military habits—despotic in his ordinary demeanour—known to have scoffed in private at the principles of liberty—when such a man is seen to mount the hobby horse of popularity—to join in the cry of danger to liberty—to take every opportunity of embarrassing the General Government & bringing it under suspicion—to flatter and fall in with all the non sense of the zealots of the day—It may justly be suspected that his object is to throw things into confusion that he may "ride the storm and direct the whirlwind."

It has aptly been observed that *Cato* was the Tory-*Cæsar* the Whig of his day. The former frequently resisted—the latter always flattered the follies of the people. Yet the former perished with the Republic the latter destroyed it.

No popular Government was ever without its Catalines & its Cæsars. These are its true enemies. [this reference is from the play, Cato, by Joseph Addison, 1712]

As far as I am informed the anxiety of those who are calumniated is to keep the Government in the state in which it is, which they fear will be no easy task, from a natural tendency in the state of things to exalt the local on the ruins of the National Government. Some of them appear to wish, in a constitutional way, a change in the judiciary department of the Government, from an apprehension that an orderly and effectual administration of Justice cannot be obtained without a more intimate connection between the state and national Tribunals. But even this is not an object of any set of men as a party. There is a difference of opinion about it on various grounds among those who have generally acted together. As to any other change of consequence, I believe nobody dreams of it.

Tis curious to observe the anticipations of the different parties. One side appears to believe that there is a serious plot to overturn the state Governments and substitute monarchy to the present republican system. The other side firmly believes that there is a serious plot to overturn the General Government & elevate the separate power of the states upon its ruins. Both sides may be equally wrong & their mutual jealousies may be materially causes of the appearances which mutually disturb them, and sharpen them against each other…

This is a palpable misrepresentation. No man, that I know of, contemplated the introducing into this country of a monarchy. A very small number (not more than three or four) manifested theoretical opinions favourable in the abstract to a constitution like that of Great Britain, but every one agreed that such a constitution except as to the general distribution of departments and powers was out of the Question in reference to this Country. The Member who was most explicit on this point (a Member from New York) declared in strong terms that the *republican theory ought to be adhered to in this Country as long as there was any chance of its success—that the idea of a perfect equality of political rights among the citizens, exclusive of all permanent or hereditary distinctions, was of a nature to engage the good wishes of every good man,* whatever might be his theoretic doubts—that it merited his best efforts to give success to it in practice—that hitherto from an incompetent structure of the Government it had not had a fair trial, and that the endeavour ought then to be to secure to it a better chance of success by a government more capable of energy and order."

[Emphasis, mine]

The Constitution of the United States: A Transcription

[This and The Bill of Rights taken from the National Archives website]

[Note: The following text is a transcription of the Constitution as it was inscribed by Jacob Shallus on parchment (the document on display in the Rotunda at the National Archives Museum.) *The spelling and punctuation reflect the original.]*

We the People of the United States, in Order to form a more perfect Union, establish Justice, insure domestic Tranquility, provide for the common defence, promote the general Welfare, and secure the Blessings of Liberty to ourselves and our Posterity, do ordain and establish this Constitution for the United States of America.

Article. I.

Section. 1.

All legislative Powers herein granted shall be vested in a Congress of the United States, which shall consist of a Senate and House of Representatives.

Section. 2.

The House of Representatives shall be composed of Members chosen every second Year by the People of the several States, and the Electors in each State shall have the Qualifications requisite for Electors of the most numerous Branch of the State Legislature.

No Person shall be a Representative who shall not have attained to the Age of twenty five Years, and been seven Years a Citizen of the United States, and who shall not, when elected, be an Inhabitant of that State in which he shall be chosen.

Representatives and direct Taxes shall be apportioned among the several States which may be included within this Union, according to their respective Numbers, which shall be determined by adding to the whole Number of free Persons, including those bound to Service for a Term of Years, and excluding Indians not taxed, three fifths of all other Persons. The actual Enumeration shall be made within three Years after the first Meeting of the Congress of the United States, and within every subsequent Term of ten Years, in such Manner as they shall by Law direct. The Number of Representatives shall not exceed one for every thirty Thousand, but each State shall have at Least one Representative; and until such enumeration shall be made, the State of New Hampshire shall be entitled to chuse three, Massachusetts eight, Rhode-Island and Providence Plantations one, Connecticut five, New-York six, New Jersey four, Pennsylvania eight, Delaware one, Maryland six, Virginia ten, North Carolina five, South Carolina five, and Georgia three.

When vacancies happen in the Representation from any State, the Executive Authority thereof shall issue Writs of Election to fill such Vacancies.

The House of Representatives shall chuse their Speaker and other Officers; and shall have the sole Power of Impeachment.

Section. 3.

The Senate of the United States shall be composed of two Senators from each State, chosen by the Legislature thereof, for six Years; and each Senator shall have one Vote.

Immediately after they shall be assembled in Consequence of the first Election, they shall be divided as equally as may be into three Classes. The Seats of the Senators of the first Class shall be vacated at the Expiration of the second Year, of the second Class at the Expiration of the fourth Year, and of the third Class at the Expiration of the sixth Year, so that one third may be chosen every second Year; and if Vacancies happen by Resignation, or otherwise, during the Recess of the Legislature of any State, the Executive thereof may make temporary Appointments until the next Meeting of the Legislature, which shall then fill such Vacancies.

No Person shall be a Senator who shall not have attained to the Age of thirty Years, and been nine Years a Citizen of the United States, and who shall not, when elected, be an Inhabitant of that State for which he shall be chosen.

The Vice President of the United States shall be President of the Senate, but shall have no Vote, unless they be equally divided.

The Senate shall chuse their other Officers, and also a President pro tempore, in the Absence of the Vice President, or when he shall exercise the Office of President of the United States.

The Senate shall have the sole Power to try all Impeachments. When sitting for that Purpose, they shall be on Oath or Affirmation. When the President of the United States is tried, the Chief Justice shall preside: And no Person shall be convicted without the Concurrence of two thirds of the Members present.

Judgment in Cases of Impeachment shall not extend further than to removal from Office, and disqualification to hold and enjoy any Office of honor, Trust or Profit under the United States: but the Party convicted shall nevertheless be liable and subject to Indictment, Trial, Judgment and Punishment, according to Law.

Section. 4.

The Times, Places and Manner of holding Elections for Senators and Representatives, shall be prescribed in each State by the Legislature thereof; but the Congress may at any time by Law make or alter such Regulations, except as to the Places of chusing Senators.

The Congress shall assemble at least once in every Year, and such Meeting shall be on the first Monday in December, unless they shall by Law appoint a different Day.

Section. 5.

Each House shall be the Judge of the Elections, Returns and Qualifications of its own Members, and a Majority of each shall constitute a Quorum to do Business; but a smaller Number may adjourn from day to day, and may be authorized to compel the Attendance of absent Members, in such Manner, and under such Penalties as each House may provide.

Each House may determine the Rules of its Proceedings, punish its Members for disorderly Behaviour, and, with the Concurrence of two thirds, expel a Member.

Each House shall keep a Journal of its Proceedings, and from time to time publish the same, excepting such Parts as may in their Judgment require Secrecy; and the Yeas and Nays of the Members of either House on any question shall, at the Desire of one fifth of those Present, be entered on the Journal.

Neither House, during the Session of Congress, shall, without the Consent of the other, adjourn for more than three days, nor to any other Place than that in which the two Houses shall be sitting.

Section. 6.

The Senators and Representatives shall receive a Compensation for their Services, to be ascertained by Law, and paid out of the Treasury of the United States. They shall in all Cases, except Treason, Felony and Breach of the Peace, be privileged from Arrest during their Attendance at the Session of their respective Houses, and in going to and returning from the same; and for any Speech or Debate in either House, they shall not be questioned in any other Place.

No Senator or Representative shall, during the Time for which he was elected, be appointed to any civil Office under the Authority of the United States, which shall have been created, or the Emoluments whereof shall have been encreased during such time; and no Person holding any Office under the United States, shall be a Member of either House during his Continuance in Office.

Section. 7.

All Bills for raising Revenue shall originate in the House of Representatives; but the Senate may propose or concur with Amendments as on other Bills.

Every Bill which shall have passed the House of Representatives and the Senate, shall, before it become a Law, be presented to the President of the United States; If he approve he shall sign it, but if not he shall return it, with his Objections to that House in which it shall have originated, who shall enter the Objections at large on their Journal, and proceed to reconsider it. If after such Reconsideration two thirds of that House shall agree to pass the Bill, it shall be sent, together with the Objections, to the other House, by which it shall likewise be reconsidered, and if approved by two thirds of that House, it shall become a Law. But in all such Cases the Votes of both Houses shall be determined by yeas and Nays, and the Names of the Persons voting for and against the Bill shall be entered on the Journal of each House respectively. If any Bill shall not be returned by the President within ten Days (Sundays excepted) after it shall have been presented to him, the Same shall be a Law, in like Manner as if he had signed it, unless the Congress by their Adjournment prevent its Return, in which Case it shall not be a Law.

Every Order, Resolution, or Vote to which the Concurrence of the Senate and House of Representatives may be necessary (except on a question of Adjournment) shall be presented to the President of the United States; and before the Same shall take Effect, shall be approved by him, or being disapproved by him, shall be repassed by two thirds of the Senate and House of Representatives, according to the Rules and Limitations prescribed in the Case of a Bill.

Section. 8.

The Congress shall have Power To lay and collect Taxes, Duties, Imposts and Excises, to pay the Debts and provide for the common Defence and general Welfare of the United States; but all Duties, Imposts and Excises shall be uniform throughout the United States;

To borrow Money on the credit of the United States;

To regulate Commerce with foreign Nations, and among the several States, and with the Indian Tribes;

To establish an uniform Rule of Naturalization, and uniform Laws on the subject of Bankruptcies throughout the United States;

To coin Money, regulate the Value thereof, and of foreign Coin, and fix the Standard of Weights and Measures;

To provide for the Punishment of counterfeiting the Securities and current Coin of the United States;

To establish Post Offices and post Roads;

To promote the Progress of Science and useful Arts, by securing for limited Times to Authors and Inventors the exclusive Right to their respective Writings and Discoveries;

To constitute Tribunals inferior to the supreme Court;

To define and punish Piracies and Felonies committed on the high Seas, and Offences against the Law of Nations;

To declare War, grant Letters of Marque and Reprisal, and make Rules concerning Captures on Land and Water;

To raise and support Armies, but no Appropriation of Money to that Use shall be for a longer Term than two Years;

To provide and maintain a Navy;

To make Rules for the Government and Regulation of the land and naval Forces;

To provide for calling forth the Militia to execute the Laws of the Union, suppress Insurrections and repel Invasions;

To provide for organizing, arming, and disciplining, the Militia, and for governing such Part of them as may be employed in the Service of the United States, reserving to the States respectively, the Appointment of the Officers, and the Authority of training the Militia according to the discipline prescribed by Congress;

To exercise exclusive Legislation in all Cases whatsoever, over such District (not exceeding ten Miles square) as may, by Cession of particular States, and the Acceptance of Congress, become the Seat of the Government of the United States, and to exercise like Authority over all Places purchased by the Consent of the Legislature of the State in which the Same shall be, for the Erection of Forts, Magazines, Arsenals, dock-Yards, and other needful Buildings;—And

To make all Laws which shall be necessary and proper for carrying into Execution the foregoing Powers, and all other Powers vested by this Constitution in the Government of the United States, or in any Department or Officer thereof.

Section. 9.

The Migration or Importation of such Persons as any of the States now existing shall think proper to admit, shall not be prohibited by the Congress prior to the Year one thousand eight hundred and eight, but a Tax or duty may be imposed on such Importation, not exceeding ten dollars for each Person.

The Privilege of the Writ of Habeas Corpus shall not be suspended, unless when in Cases of Rebellion or Invasion the public Safety may require it.

No Bill of Attainder or ex post facto Law shall be passed.

No Capitation, or other direct, Tax shall be laid, unless in Proportion to the Census or enumeration herein before directed to be taken.

No Tax or Duty shall be laid on Articles exported from any State.

No Preference shall be given by any Regulation of Commerce or Revenue to the Ports of one State over those of another: nor shall Vessels bound to, or from, one State, be obliged to enter, clear, or pay Duties in another.

No Money shall be drawn from the Treasury, but in Consequence of Appropriations made by Law; and a regular Statement and Account of the Receipts and Expenditures of all public Money shall be published from time to time.

No Title of Nobility shall be granted by the United States: And no Person holding any Office of Profit or Trust under them, shall, without the Consent of the Congress, accept of any present, Emolument, Office, or Title, of any kind whatever, from any King, Prince, or foreign State.

Section. 10.

No State shall enter into any Treaty, Alliance, or Confederation; grant Letters of Marque and Reprisal; coin Money; emit Bills of Credit; make any Thing but gold and silver Coin a Tender in Payment of Debts; pass any Bill of Attainder, ex post facto Law, or Law impairing the Obligation of Contracts, or grant any Title of Nobility.

No State shall, without the Consent of the Congress, lay any Imposts or Duties on Imports or Exports, except what may be absolutely necessary for executing it's inspection Laws: and the net Produce of all Duties and Imposts, laid by any State on

Imports or Exports, shall be for the Use of the Treasury of the United States; and all such Laws shall be subject to the Revision and Controul of the Congress.

No State shall, without the Consent of Congress, lay any Duty of Tonnage, keep Troops, or Ships of War in time of Peace, enter into any Agreement or Compact with another State, or with a foreign Power, or engage in War, unless actually invaded, or in such imminent Danger as will not admit of delay.

Article. II.

Section. 1.

The executive Power shall be vested in a President of the United States of America. He shall hold his Office during the Term of four Years, and, together with the Vice President, chosen for the same Term, be elected, as follows

Each State shall appoint, in such Manner as the Legislature thereof may direct, a Number of Electors, equal to the whole Number of Senators and Representatives to which the State may be entitled in the Congress: but no Senator or Representative, or Person holding an Office of Trust or Profit under the United States, shall be appointed an Elector.

The Electors shall meet in their respective States, and vote by Ballot for two Persons, of whom one at least shall not be an Inhabitant of the same State with themselves. And they shall make a List of all the Persons voted for, and of the Number of Votes for each; which List they shall sign and certify, and transmit sealed to the Seat of the Government of the United States, directed to the President of the Senate. The President of the Senate shall, in the Presence of the Senate and House of

Representatives, open all the Certificates, and the Votes shall then be counted. The Person having the greatest Number of Votes shall be the President, if such Number be a Majority of the whole Number of Electors appointed; and if there be more than one who have such Majority, and have an equal Number of Votes, then the House of Representatives shall immediately chuse by Ballot one of them for President; and if no Person have a Majority, then from the five highest on the List the said House shall in like Manner chuse the President. But in chusing the President, the Votes shall be taken by States, the Representation from each State having one Vote; A quorum for this Purpose shall consist of a Member or Members from two thirds of the States, and a Majority of all the States shall be necessary to a Choice. In every Case, after the Choice of the President, the Person having the greatest Number of Votes of the Electors shall be the Vice President. But if there should remain two or more who have equal Votes, the Senate shall chuse from them by Ballot the Vice President.

The Congress may determine the Time of chusing the Electors, and the Day on which they shall give their Votes; which Day shall be the same throughout the United States.

No Person except a natural born Citizen, or a Citizen of the United States, at the time of the Adoption of this Constitution, shall be eligible to the Office of President; neither shall any Person be eligible to that Office who shall not have attained to the Age of thirty five Years, and been fourteen Years a Resident within the United States.

In Case of the Removal of the President from Office, or of his Death, Resignation, or Inability to discharge the Powers and Duties of the said Office, the Same shall devolve on the Vice

President, and the Congress may by Law provide for the Case of Removal, Death, Resignation or Inability, both of the President and Vice President, declaring what Officer shall then act as President, and such Officer shall act accordingly, until the Disability be removed, or a President shall be elected.

The President shall, at stated Times, receive for his Services, a Compensation, which shall neither be encreased nor diminished during the Period for which he shall have been elected, and he shall not receive within that Period any other Emolument from the United States, or any of them.

Before he enter on the Execution of his Office, he shall take the following Oath or Affirmation:—"I do solemnly swear (or affirm) that I will faithfully execute the Office of President of the United States, and will to the best of my Ability, preserve, protect and defend the Constitution of the United States."

Section. 2.

The President shall be Commander in Chief of the Army and Navy of the United States, and of the Militia of the several States, when called into the actual Service of the United States; he may require the Opinion, in writing, of the principal Officer in each of the executive Departments, upon any Subject relating to the Duties of their respective Offices, and he shall have Power to grant Reprieves and Pardons for Offences against the United States, except in Cases of Impeachment.

He shall have Power, by and with the Advice and Consent of the Senate, to make Treaties, provided two thirds of the Senators present concur; and he shall nominate, and by and with the Advice and Consent of the Senate, shall appoint Ambassadors, other public Ministers and Consuls, Judges of the supreme Court, and all other Officers of the United States, whose Appointments are not herein otherwise provided for, and which shall be established by Law: but the Congress may by Law vest the Appointment of such inferior Officers, as they think proper, in the President alone, in the Courts of Law, or in the Heads of Departments.

The President shall have Power to fill up all Vacancies that may happen during the Recess of the Senate, by granting Commissions which shall expire at the End of their next Session.

Section. 3.

He shall from time to time give to the Congress Information of the State of the Union, and recommend to their Consideration such Measures as he shall judge necessary and expedient; he may, on extraordinary Occasions, convene both Houses, or either of them, and in Case of Disagreement between them, with Respect to the Time of Adjournment, he may adjourn them to such Time as he shall think proper; he shall receive Ambassadors and other public Ministers; he shall take Care that the Laws be faithfully executed, and shall Commission all the Officers of the United States.

Section. 4.

The President, Vice President and all civil Officers of the United States, shall be removed from Office on Impeachment for, and Conviction of, Treason, Bribery, or other high Crimes and Misdemeanors.

Article III.

Section. 1.

The judicial Power of the United States, shall be vested in one supreme Court, and in such inferior Courts as the Congress may from time to time ordain and establish. The Judges, both of the supreme and inferior Courts, shall hold their Offices during good Behaviour, and shall, at stated Times, receive for their Services, a Compensation, which shall not be diminished during their Continuance in Office.

Section. 2.

The judicial Power shall extend to all Cases, in Law and Equity, arising under this Constitution, the Laws of the United States, and Treaties made, or which shall be made, under their Authority;—to all Cases affecting Ambassadors, other public Ministers and Consuls;—to all Cases of admiralty and maritime Jurisdiction;—to Controversies to which the United States shall be a Party;—to Controversies between two or more States;—between a State and Citizens of another State,—between Citizens of different States,—between Citizens of the same State claiming Lands under Grants of different States, and between a State, or the Citizens thereof, and foreign States, Citizens or Subjects.

In all Cases affecting Ambassadors, other public Ministers and Consuls, and those in which a State shall be Party, the supreme Court shall have original Jurisdiction. In all the other Cases before mentioned, the supreme Court shall have appellate Jurisdiction, both as to Law and Fact, with such Exceptions, and under such Regulations as the Congress shall make.

The Trial of all Crimes, except in Cases of Impeachment, shall be by Jury; and such Trial shall be held in the State where the said Crimes shall have been committed; but when not committed within any State, the Trial shall be at such Place or Places as the Congress may by Law have directed.

Section. 3.

Treason against the United States, shall consist only in levying War against them, or in adhering to their Enemies, giving them Aid and Comfort. No Person shall be convicted of Treason unless on the Testimony of two Witnesses to the same overt Act, or on Confession in open Court.

The Congress shall have Power to declare the Punishment of Treason, but no Attainder of Treason shall work Corruption of Blood, or Forfeiture except during the Life of the Person attainted.

Article. IV.

Section. 1.

Full Faith and Credit shall be given in each State to the public Acts, Records, and judicial Proceedings of every other State. And the Congress may by general Laws prescribe the Manner in which such Acts, Records and Proceedings shall be proved, and the Effect thereof.

Section. 2.

The Citizens of each State shall be entitled to all Privileges and Immunities of Citizens in the several States.

A Person charged in any State with Treason, Felony, or other Crime, who shall flee from Justice, and be found in another State, shall on Demand of the executive Authority of the State from which he fled, be delivered up, to be removed to the State having Jurisdiction of the Crime.

No Person held to Service or Labour in one State, under the Laws thereof, escaping into another, shall, in Consequence of any Law or Regulation therein, be discharged from such Service or Labour, but shall be delivered up on Claim of the Party to whom such Service or Labour may be due.

Section. 3.

New States may be admitted by the Congress into this Union; but no new State shall be formed or erected within the Jurisdiction of any other State; nor any State be formed by the Junction of two or more States, or Parts of States, without the Consent of the Legislatures of the States concerned as well as of the Congress.

The Congress shall have Power to dispose of and make all needful Rules and Regulations respecting the Territory or other Property belonging to the United States; and nothing in this Constitution shall be so construed as to Prejudice any Claims of the United States, or of any particular State.

Section. 4.

The United States shall guarantee to every State in this Union a Republican Form of Government, and shall protect each of them against Invasion; and on Application of the Legislature, or of the Executive (when the Legislature cannot be convened), against domestic Violence.

Article. V.

The Congress, whenever two thirds of both Houses shall deem it necessary, shall propose Amendments to this Constitution, or, on the Application of the Legislatures of two thirds of the several States, shall call a Convention for proposing Amendments, which, in either Case, shall be valid to all Intents and Purposes, as Part of this Constitution, when ratified by the Legislatures of three fourths of the several States, or by Conventions in three fourths thereof, as the one or the other Mode of Ratification may be proposed by the Congress; Provided that no Amendment which may be made prior to the Year One thousand eight hundred and eight shall in any Manner affect the first and fourth Clauses in the Ninth Section of the first Article; and that no State, without its Consent, shall be deprived of its equal Suffrage in the Senate.

Article. VI.

All Debts contracted and Engagements entered into, before the Adoption of this Constitution, shall be as valid against the United States under this Constitution, as under the Confederation.

This Constitution, and the Laws of the United States which shall be made in Pursuance thereof; and all Treaties made, or which shall be made, under the Authority of the United States, shall be the supreme Law of the Land; and the Judges in every State shall be bound thereby, any Thing in the Constitution or Laws of any State to the Contrary notwithstanding.

The Senators and Representatives before mentioned, and the Members of the several State Legislatures, and all executive and judicial Officers, both of the United States and of the several States, shall be bound by Oath or Affirmation, to support this Constitution; but no religious Test shall ever be required as a Qualification to any Office or public Trust under the United States.

Article. VII.

The Ratification of the Conventions of nine States, shall be sufficient for the Establishment of this Constitution between the States so ratifying the Same.

The Word, "the," being interlined between the seventh and eighth Lines of the first Page, The Word "Thirty" being partly written on an Erazure in the fifteenth Line of the first Page, The Words "is tried" being interlined between the thirty second and thirty third Lines of the first Page and the Word "the" being interlined between the forty third and forty fourth Lines of the second Page.

Attest William Jackson Secretary

done in Convention by the Unanimous Consent of the States present the Seventeenth Day of September in the Year of our Lord one thousand seven hundred and Eighty seven and of the Independance of the United States of America the Twelfth In witness whereof We have hereunto subscribed our Names,

[Signatures not included]

The U.S. Bill of Rights

The Preamble to The Bill of Rights

Congress of the United States
begun and held at the City of New-York, on
Wednesday the fourth of March, one thousand seven hundred and eighty nine.

THE Conventions of a number of the States, having at the time of their adopting the Constitution, expressed a desire, in order to prevent misconstruction or abuse of its powers, that further declaratory and restrictive clauses should be added: And as extending the ground of public confidence in the Government, will best ensure the beneficent ends of its institution.

RESOLVED by the Senate and House of Representatives of the United States of America, in Congress assembled, two thirds of both Houses concurring, that the following Articles be proposed to the Legislatures of the several States, as amendments to the Constitution of the United States, all, or any of which Articles, when ratified by three fourths of the said Legislatures, to be valid to all intents and purposes, as part of the said Constitution; viz.

ARTICLES in addition to, and Amendment of the Constitution of the United States of America, proposed by Congress, and ratified by the Legislatures of the several States, pursuant to the fifth Article of the original Constitution.

[**Note:** The following text is a transcription of the first ten amendments to the Constitution in their original form. These amendments were ratified December 15, 1791, and form what is known as the "Bill of Rights."]

Amendment I

Congress shall make no law respecting an establishment of religion, or prohibiting the free exercise thereof; or abridging the freedom of speech, or of the press; or the right of the people peaceably to assemble, and to petition the Government for a redress of grievances.

Amendment II

A well regulated Militia, being necessary to the security of a free State, the right of the people to keep and bear Arms, shall not be infringed.

Amendment III

No Soldier shall, in time of peace be quartered in any house, without the consent of the Owner, nor in time of war, but in a manner to be prescribed by law.

Amendment IV

The right of the people to be secure in their persons, houses, papers, and effects, against unreasonable searches and seizures, shall not be violated, and no Warrants shall issue, but upon probable cause, supported by Oath or affirmation, and particularly describing the place to be searched, and the persons or things to be seized.

Amendment V

No person shall be held to answer for a capital, or otherwise infamous crime, unless on a presentment or indictment of a Grand Jury, except in cases arising in the land or naval forces, or in the Militia, when in actual service in time of War or public danger; nor shall any person be subject for the same offence to be twice put in jeopardy of life or limb; nor shall be compelled in any criminal case to be a witness against himself, nor be deprived of life, liberty, or property, without due process of law; nor shall private property be taken for public use, without just compensation.

Amendment VI

In all criminal prosecutions, the accused shall enjoy the right to a speedy and public trial, by an impartial jury of the State and district wherein the crime shall have been committed, which district shall have been previously ascertained by law, and to be informed of the nature and cause of the accusation; to be confronted with the witnesses against him; to have compulsory process for obtaining witnesses in his favor, and to have the Assistance of Counsel for his defence.

Amendment VII

In Suits at common law, where the value in controversy shall exceed twenty dollars, the right of trial by jury shall be preserved, and no fact tried by a jury, shall be otherwise re-examined in any Court of the United States, than according to the rules of the common law.

Amendment VIII

Excessive bail shall not be required, nor excessive fines imposed, nor cruel and unusual punishments inflicted.

Amendment IX

The enumeration in the Constitution, of certain rights, shall not be construed to deny or disparage others retained by the people.

Amendment X

The powers not delegated to the United States by the Constitution, nor prohibited by it to the States, are reserved to the States respectively, or to the people.

BIBLIOGRAPHY

Introduction

Fox News, edited Sept. 20, 2018, https://en.wikipedia.org/wiki/Fox_News

Conservative Review, edited Sept. 23, 2018, https://en.wikipedia.org/wiki/Conservative_Review

Conservative Talk Radio, edited Sept 18, 2018 https://en.wikipedia.org/wiki/Conservative_talk_radio

John Birch Society, edited Sept 18, 2018 https://en.wikipedia.org/wiki/John_Birch_Society

Libertarianism, edited September 22, 2018, https://en.wikipedia.org/wiki/Libertarianism

Reardon, Kathleen, Updated December 17 2011, *The High Political Price of "Some Say" Journalism*, https://www.huffingtonpost.com/kathleen-reardon/the-high-political-price_b_1015843.html

Crouch, Morgan, Updated June 25 2018, What Are the Seven Techniques of Propaganda? https://classroom.synonym.com/what-are-the-seven-techniques-of-propaganda-12080912.html

Reich, Robert, March 06, 2019, *Win-at-any-cost mentality is eroding American life*, https://chicago.suntimes.com/opinion/win-at-any-cost-mentality-is-eroding-american-life/

Fake News, edited September 19, 2018, https://en.wikipedia.org/wiki/Fake_news

Fox, Maggie, March 08, 2018, *Fake News: Lies spread faster on social media than truth does*, https://www.nbcnews.com/health/health-news/fake-news-lies-spread-faster-social-media-truth-does-n854896

All Men are Created Equal, edited September 14, 2018, https://en.wikipedia.org/wiki/All_men_are_created_equal

Nineteen Eighty-Four, edited September 20, 2018, https://en.wikipedia.org/wiki/Nineteen_Eighty-Four

Republic, edited September 23, 2018, https://en.wikiquote.org/wiki/Republic

Chapter One

Translated by Benjamen Jowett; *The Republic* by Plato, http://classics.mit.edu/Plato/republic.html

1776, by David McCollough; New York, Simon and Schuster, 2006, print.

Cothran, Martin, *Classical Education of the Founding* Fathers, April 15, 2007 https://www.memoriapress.com/articles/classical-education-founding-fathers/

Special Readings in American Politics, Editors W.B. Stubbs and C.B. Gosnel; New York, Charles Schribner's Sons, 1947, print

Sabo, Mike, April 28, 2018, *The American Founders Knew A Virtuous Republic Requires Virtuous People* http://thefederalist.com/2017/04/28/the-american-founders-knew-a-virtuous-republic-requires-virtuous-people/

Cato, A Tragedy; edited September 17, 2018, https://en.wikipedia.org/wiki/Cato,_a_Tragedy

Religion in Colonial America: Trends, Regulations, and Beliefs; (no editing date given), https://www.facinghistory.org/nobigotry/religion-colonial-america-trends-regulations-and-beliefs

Separation of Church and State; edited October 1, 2018 https://en.wikipedia.org/wiki/Separation_of_church_and_state_in_the_United_States

Grannon, Cydney; *What's the Difference Between Ethics and Morality?*; (no editing date given) https://www.britannica.com/story/whats-the-difference-between-morality-and-ethics

Chapter Two

Translated by Benjamen Jowett; *The Republic* by Plato, http://classics.mit.edu/Plato/republic.html

Direct Democracy, edited September 22, 2018, https://en.wikipedia.org/wiki/Direct_democracy

Republic, edited September 23, 2018, https://en.wikipedia.org/wiki/Republic

Pluralistic Democracy, edited September 11, 2018 https://en.wikipedia.org/wiki/Pluralist_democracy

Meacham, John, *Thomas Jefferson, The Art of Power*, New York, Random House, 2012

Chapter Three

Siegler, Kirk; *Alt-Right Groups Splinter, Distance From White Supremacy*; August 11, 2018 http://www.southcarolinapublicradio.org/post/after-charlottesville-alt-right-groups-splinter-distance-white-supremacy

Semantics, edited September 17, 2018, https://en.wikipedia.org/wiki/Semantics

Democratic Party (United States), edited September 22, 2018, https://en.wikipedia.org/wiki/Democratic_Party_(United_States)

Republican Party (United States), edited September 22, 2018, https://en.wikipedia.org/wiki/Republican_Party_(United_States)

Howard Means; *Andrew Johnson, the Avenger Takes His Place*, Orlando, FL, Houghton Mifflin Harcourt 2006

Federalist Party, edited September 22, 2018, https://en.wikipedia.org/wiki/Federalist_Party

Libertarianism, edited September 22, 2018, https://en.wikipedia.org/wiki/Libertarianism

Tea Party Movement, edited September 30, 2018 https://en.wikipedia.org/wiki/Tea_Party_movement

Reaganomics, edited October 2, 2018 https://en.wikipedia.org/wiki/Reaganomics

Beattie, Alan, *False Economy*, Riverhead Books, New York, 2009

Chapter Four

Lendman, Steven, June 8, 2010, *Fleecing of America,* *https://rense.com/general83/fleec.htm*

Electing the President: Voter Apathy, copyright 2018 https://historynewsnetwork.org/article/146517

The Great Depression, edited September 17, 2018 *https://en.wikipedia.org/wiki/Great_Depression*

10 of the most Lethal CIA Interventions in Latin America, September 18, 2016, https://www.telesurtv.net/english/analysis/10-of-the-Most-

Lethal-CIA-Interventions-in-Latin-America-20160608-0031.html

Issacs, Arnold, *American has One War it Just Keeps Losing, https://www.thenation.com/article/america-just-has-one-war-that-it-keeps-losing/*

Grover Norquist, edited September 22, 2018, https://en.wikipedia.org/wiki/Grover_Norquist

Dellinger, Matt, and John Cassidy, August 01, 2008, *Wednesdays with Grover*, https://www.newyorker.com/magazine/2005/08/01/wednesdays-with-grover

Grover Norquist on Gerrymandering, November 12 to Novermber 14, 2016, Twitter threads, https://twitter.com/GroverNorquist/status/797488290605789185

Iraq War Media Reporting, Journalism and Propaganda, August 01, 2007, http://www.globalissues.org/article/461/media-reporting-journalism-and-propaganda#WarReportingandJournalism

Propaganda Techniques July 23, 2018 https://en.wikipedia.org/wiki/Propaganda_techniques

Chapter Five

Langone, Alix, August 14, 2018 *An 11-Year-Old Hacked Into a U.S. Voting System Replica in 10 Minutes This Weekend* http://time.com/5366171/11-year-old-hacked-into-us-voting-system-10-minutes/

Why American elections cost so much
https://www.economist.com/the-economist-explains/2014/02/09/why-american-elections-cost-so-much

Raphelson, Samantha, July 18, 2018; *Muslim Americans Running For Office In Highest Numbers Since 2001*
https://www.npr.org/2018/07/18/630132952/muslim-americans-running-for-office-in-highest-numbers-since-2001

Levine, Mark, December 19, 2004*, Did a Republican Congressman Rig the 2004 election?* , podcast
http://www.marklevinetalk.com/did-a-republican-congressman-rig-the-2004-election/

Sager, Josh, *Monsanto Controls Both the White House and the US Congress*, March 08, 2018
https://www.globalresearch.ca/monsanto-controls-both-the-white-house-and-the-us-congress/5336422

Chapter Six

Paine, Thomas, Common Sense, January 10, 1776
https://en.wikipedia.org/wiki/Common_Sense_(pamphlet)

Clark, Kenneth, February 23 to May 18th, 1969; *Civilisation*, TV series, BBC
https://en.wikipedia.org/wiki/Civilisation_(TV_series)

Appendix

Miller, Clyde, *Special Readings in American Politics*, Editors W.B. Stubbs and C.B. Gosnel; New York, Charles Schribner's Sons, 1947, print pp. 321-326

Crouch, Morgan, Updated June 25 2018, What Are the Seven Techniques of Propaganda? [with comments] https://classroom.synonym.com/what-are-the-seven-techniques-of-propaganda-12080912.html

Propaganda Techniques July 23, 2018 https://en.wikipedia.org/wiki/Propaganda_techniques

Alexander Hamilton, *Enclosure: [Objections and Answers Respecting the Administration], [18 August 1792],* from the Hamilton papers, National Archives, Library of Congress https://founders.archives.gov/documents/Hamilton/01-12-02-0184-0002

The Constitution of The United States of America ; The National Archives https://www.archives.gov/founding-docs/constitution-transcript

The Bill of Rights; The National Archives https://www.archives.gov/founding-docs/bill-of-rights-transcript

NOTES

NOTES

NOTES

www.ingramcontent.com/pod-product-compliance
Lightning Source LLC
Chambersburg PA
CBHW031310250726
48656CB00005B/1729

* 9 7 8 1 7 2 4 0 9 8 8 0 1 *